Upgrade Your
A · R · M · Y
DISCHARGE

Michael Waddington

Upgrade Your Army Discharge: A Brief Legal Guide
COPYRIGHT © 2011 Michael Waddington

Published by:
Michael Waddington
601 North Belair Square, Suite 16
Evans, GA 30802
United States of America

LegalNichePros.com

ISBN-13:
978-0984720002 (Legal Niche Pros, LLC)

ISBN-10:
0984720006

Contents

Disclaimer

This book was written to provide information to help you learn about the Army discharge upgrade process. Every effort has been made to make this book as complete and accurate as possible. However, there may be mistakes or omissions in typography or content. Also, this book contains information on upgrading Army discharges only up to the publishing date. Therefore, this report should be used only as a guide – not as the ultimate source of Army discharge upgrade information.

The purpose of this book is to educate. Neither the author nor publisher warrants that the information contained in this book is fully complete and neither shall not be responsible for any errors or omissions. The author and publisher shall have neither liability nor responsibility to any person or entity with respect to any loss or damage caused or alleged to be caused directly or indirectly by this book.

Note from the Author:

My goal in creating this ebook is to make it a primary reference for people to use for assistance in upgrading their discharges, particularly those people who do not have the money to hire a competent lawyer.

I am a court martial lawyer and my site is ucmjdefense.com.

I get a lot of calls inquiring about discharge upgrades, but with my case load, I just don't have the time to help everyone. I thought a good ebook explaining the discharge upgrade processes, when to use each process, and how to apply for a discharge upgrade would be helpful for anyone looking to upgrade.

Introduction

Title 10, United States Code, Section 1553, authorizes the Secretary of the Army to establish a board of review serving the Army, Army Reserve, and National Guard for the purpose of upgrading discharges and changing records. The U.S Code does not allow the boards to revoke a discharge or recall a person to active duty - only to change an existing discharge or to correct an error or injustice.

When you apply to have a discharge upgraded through the Army Discharge Review Board, you are doing so on the basis that your current discharge was either inequitable or improper – that's it.

If you apply to the Army Board of Corrections of Military Records, your basis for doing so is your discovery of an error or injustice that you are seeking to get corrected, or your discharge upgrade request at the Army Discharge Review Board was not approved and you are applying to this Board as an appeal. And with either board, success doesn't come easy.

Only about 41 percent of Army Discharge Review Board applications result in a discharge upgrade, and only about 10 to 15 percent of the Army Board of Corrections of Military Records applications are successful. Requesting counsel representation and your personal appearance help increase your chances at getting an upgrade approved, but success is never guaranteed nor automatic.

Inequitable means the discharge you received was too severe for the action or event causing the discharge. *Improper* means the Army did not follow its own established procedures when they considered your discharge.

It is up to you to justify why your discharge rating should be changed.

The Army has two different kinds of Boards to review applications:

- The Army Discharge Review Board
- The Army Board of Corrections of Military Records

Each Board serves a different purpose and uses a different form as part of its application process, and each has a different operational timeline and its own adjudication process. To apply to the Army Discharge Review Board, you must have been discharged less than 15 years from the date of your application. This timeline is not waiverable; if you are over the 15-year deadline, or you are trying to get an error or injustice corrected, then you must apply to the Army Board of Corrections to Military Records to have your records changed.

A discharge upgrade application to the Army Discharge Review Board starts with your filling out DD Form 293. The Army Discharge Review Board's only function is to review cases for discharge upgrades. The outcome will be one of two. Either your discharge will remain the same or it will be upgraded. The Board cannot change your discharge to a lower rating. You can either have a records review or you can request to appear in person with or without representation.

On the other hand, to apply to the Army Board of Corrections of Military Records, you can be over fifteen years from your date of discharge, but generally have to be within three years of when you discovered the error or injustice in your records. Applying to this board can also be your next step if your application to the Army Discharge Review Board was not approved, or if your record needs to be changed for some reason, as this board has much more power than the Army Discharge Review Board. Application to the Army Board of Corrections of Military Records starts with filling out DD Form 149.

Myths about Discharges

Many times, soldiers don't think the discharge they receive is of any real importance because it will get changed anyway. Because of this indifference, many soldiers accept whatever discharge they are given just to get out of the Army, thinking the discharge will be upgraded at a later date. That could not be further from the truth. So here are two of the prevalent myths soldiers continue to believe:

Myth #1 – "It doesn't make any difference what discharge I get, it will be upgraded to Honorable in six months anyway."

Fact – No, your discharge will not be automatically upgraded in six months – or ever. That rumor has perpetuated itself since 1979. Up to 1975, many of the less than Honorable discharges given out were based on urinalysis tests soldiers were compelled to take either to determine if they needed to be entered into a drug rehabilitation program, or if they already were in a program, to monitor their progress.

In 1979, using those tests as evidence for a less than Honorable discharge was deemed illegal. The courts ruled that the Army could discharge soldiers based on failed tests, but they could no longer give the characterization of service they had been giving.

Therefore, starting in 1979, the discharges that had been given out using the illegal process were automatically upgraded to Honorable to correct the injustice that had been done. Ever since then, the myth has continued, even though less than Honorable recipients get a fact sheet telling them of the timelines and processes available to request an upgrade.

Myth #2 – A good post-service record will assure a discharge upgrade.

Fact – While a good post-service record serves as good justification for an upgrade, an upgrade is not assured from that evidence alone.

Types of Discharges and Involuntary Separations

There are two basic types of discharges - Punitive and Administrative Separations.

Punitive Discharges. Punitive discharges are issued as part of a court-martial sentencing of a UCMJ violation. Punitive discharges come in two types:

- Dishonorable Discharge (DD) - which can be issued only by a general court-martial and is a separation under dishonorable conditions;
- Bad-Conduct Discharge (BCD) - which can be issued by either a general court-martial or a special court-martial and is a separation under conditions other than honorable.

Involuntary Administrative Separations: On the other hand, involuntary administrative separations cannot be awarded by a court-martial, are not punitive in nature, and are issued as a result of a "basis" from a list of several. For enlisted personnel, the involuntary administrative separation most likely will also have a characterization of service associated with it. There are a couple of separations that do not have characterizations attached to them.

The "basis" is the reason the soldier is being separated, while the characterization of service refers to the performance of duty and is usually deemed as Honorable, General, or Other Than Honorable.

There are several reasons a soldier could be processed for an involuntary administrative separation. The most common reasons are:

Parenthood – Generally speaking, the individual does not have a family support plan stating who will take their children, if the individual should deploy or leave home for an extended period of time. Because no plan is in place, and the parent has not designated anyone to take the children, the individual is deemed unable to satisfactorily perform duties and is therefore considered un-deployable. Before a separation basis is issued, the individual must first have been counseled about these deficiencies and provided ample opportunity to correct them.

Physical or Mental Condition – This basis is rooted on a physical or mental condition that inhibits the soldier from performing duties satisfactorily, but the condition is not severe enough to warrant a disability separation. Common examples are:

- chronic seasickness or airsickness;
- enuresis (bedwetting);
- personality disorder.

Separation on the basis of personality disorder is authorized only if the diagnosis is by a psychiatrist or psychologist, completed in accordance with procedures established by the Army, and concludes that the disorder is so severe the servicemember's ability to function effectively in the Army's military environment is significantly impaired.

Disability – A disability separation usually results in an honorable or entry level separation.

Minority Enlistment - Usually the member was under age 18 at the time of enlistment and enlisted without a parent's or guardian's permission or lied about his/her age. **Such** Minority Enlistment Discharges are normally characterized as entry level separations.

Erroneous Enlistment – When this basis occurs, it is usually not due to fraudulent conduct of the individual (as in a Minority Enlistment basis) and is most likely due to enlistment directives not being followed by a recruiter. This basis normally receives an honorable discharge or an entry level separation, if military service was less than 180 days.

Fraudulent Entry into the Military Service – This basis involves fraudulent enlistment based on deliberate material misrepresentation, omission, or concealment by the individual that if it were known, might have resulted in a rejection of enlistment. If the fraud involves a prior less than honorable period of service, the characterization issued is normally under other than honorable conditions.

Unsatisfactory Performance – Usually this basis means the individual has been found unqualified to perform military service satisfactorily. The service is normally characterized as honorable or general.

Homosexual Conduct - Homosexual conduct is grounds for separation and includes:

- homosexual acts;

- a statement by an individual with intent to engage in homosexual acts;
- homosexual marriage or attempted marriage.

When the sole basis for separation is homosexual conduct, a characterization under other than honorable conditions may be issued, but only if there is a finding that during the current term of service the member attempted, solicited, or committed a homosexual act.

Homosexual Conduct, as the basis for an Involuntary Administrative Separation, entitles the soldier to an Administrative Discharge Board, regardless of characterization or time-in-service.

Alcohol Abuse Rehabilitation Failure – Separation may occur for a member who has been referred to a program of rehabilitation for drug or alcohol abuse, but who fails to complete the program.

Misconduct - A member may be separated for misconduct when it is determined the member is unqualified for further military service for one or more of the following reasons:

- Minor disciplinary infractions;
- A pattern of misconduct;
- Commission of a serious offense;
- Civilian conviction.

Security - This basis is used when retaining the individual in the Army poses a national security risk the Army is not willing to take.

Unsatisfactory Participation in the Ready Reserve - A member may be separated for unsatisfactory participation in the Ready Reserve.

Weight Control Failure – An individual may be separated for failure to meet the weight control standards and is therefore unqualified for further military service.

If the soldier's weight control issue is related to a medical diagnosis, then the individual may be separated through medical channels. Characterization is usually honorable, but it can be general depending on the person's Army service record.

While these are the most common reasons, each military service has the authority to establish additional reasons for involuntary administrative discharges, based on the unique qualifications of the particular service.

In many of the reasons for separation, the member must have been formally counseled concerning the deficiencies and afforded ample opportunity to correct those deficiencies before being separated.

Certain administrative separations may be un-characterized, as in the case of a soldier separated with fewer than 180 days of service. These are also known as entry level separations.

The final type of involuntary administrative separation is called Order of Release from the Custody and Control of the Military Services and is generally issued if the enlistment or induction was not legal or didn't follow certain procedures. This type of separation also has no characterization of service associated with it.

The Involuntary Separation Process

Administrative separations fall into two categories - voluntary and involuntary. If a soldier successfully completes a contracted term of service, gets out, and has met the obligated eight years of service, it is a voluntary separation. While many people believe this will end with an honorable characterization of service, it is not guaranteed.

All administrative separations take into consideration a soldier's conduct and performance while in the Army. If the soldier had too many disciplinary actions while serving, the characterization of service could result in a general discharge. Other involuntary administrative separation reasons include:

- early release to further one's education;
- early release to accept public office;
- dependency;
- hardship;
- pregnancy or childbirth;
- conscientious objection;
- immediate reenlistment;
- separation to accept a commission;
- sole surviving family member.

The involuntary administrative discharge process begins with the soldier's commander notifying the soldier, in writing, of the proposed involuntary administrative separation proceedings. The written notice includes the basis for the separation, the worst characterization that can be applied to that basis, and the characterization the commander is recommending.

The soldier is allowed time to consult with a military attorney without cost, or with a civilian attorney at his/her own expense. The soldier may attach evidence and statements that will become part of the separation packet. If the solider has served more than six years, or if the basis is for homosexuality, or if an other than honorable characterization is recommended, then the soldier is entitled to have the case heard by an administrative discharge board.

Once the commander receives the response and attachments from the soldier, the commander determines whether or not to pursue the separation proceedings. If the commander elects to proceed and an administrative discharge board is required, then an administrative discharge board is convened. If the board is not required, the commander forwards the package to the approval authority (a higher commander) for final approval or disapproval.

The Administrative Discharge Board. The Separation Authority (the soldier's commander) appoints at least three experienced commissioned, warrant, or non-commissioned officers to the Administrative Discharge Board. Enlisted Board personnel must E-7s or above, and senior to the soldier being boarded. As a minimum, one member of the board must be an O-4 or higher, and a majority of the board must comprise commissioned or warrant officers. The senior board member serves as the Board President.

Two non-voting positions may also be filled by the Separation Authority – a recorder and a legal adviser.

If the soldier being boarded is a Reserve Component soldier (from the Army Reserve or National Guard), the board must include at least one Reserve officer as a voting member. If an other than honorable characterization is possible, all board members must be commissioned officers and senior to the soldier's reserve grade.

In every case in which characterization results in an OTH, the board proceedings must be reviewed by a judge advocate or civilian attorney employed by the Army. A review is not required when another characterization is recommended.

UPGRADE YOUR ARMY DISCHARGE

Types of Characterizations of Service

Characterization of service at separation is based upon the quality of the member's service, or in other words, how well the soldier performed while in the Army. The quality determination considers a soldier's personal conduct as well as performance of duty as found in the **Uniform Code of Military Justice (UCMJ) manual, directives and regulations,** and the time-honored customs and traditions of the Army.

Normally, a characterization of service is not determined by an isolated instance, but rather a pattern of behavior or a string of incidents. However, in certain instances, a single performance of duty incident may drive the characterization if the incident was severe. Generally though, characterizations of service fall into the following categories:

- **Honorable** - Appropriate when the soldier's quality of service generally met the standards of acceptable conduct and performance of duty. An honorable characterization recipient receives an Honorable Discharge Certificate (DD Form 256) and a notation on the DD Form 214.
- **General (Under Honorable Conditions).** Soldier had significant negative aspects in conduct or performance of duty that outweigh the positive performance. A General (Under Honorable Conditions) characterization may jeopardize a soldier's GI

17

Bill benefits. The soldier with this characterization will not be able to reenlist back into the Army or enter into another military service branch.

Under Other than Honorable Conditions. This characterization is given when a soldier's pattern of behavior significantly departs from the expected conduct. Examples may include:

- use of force or violence to produce serious bodily injury or death;
- abuse of a special position of trust;
- disregard by a superior of customary superior-subordinate relationships;
- acts or omissions endangering the security of the United States or the health and welfare of other members of the Army;
- deliberate acts or omissions that seriously endanger the health and safety of other soldiers or civilians.

An other than honorable characterization of service also carries other implications, such as:

- not entitled to retain Army uniforms or wear them home;
- accepting the mode of transportation home chosen by the Army;
- being subject to the recoupment of any reenlistment bonus;
- not being eligible for unemployment benefits;
- not paid for mileage from the place of discharge to home of record.

While many soldiers believe an other than honorable discharge renders them ineligible for all VA Benefits, this is not necessarily the case.

The VA will make its own case-by-case determination. However, most veterans' benefits will be forfeited if the soldier was involved in:

- desertion;
- escape prior to trial by general court-martial;
- a conscientious objector refusing to perform military duties;
- willful or persistent misconduct;
- offense(s) involving moral issues;
- mutiny or spying;
- homosexual acts involving aggravating circumstances.

The Army Discharge Review Board (ADRB)

Army Discharge Review Boards convene with five officers, Major/O-4 or higher. Their charge is to preside over discharges issued within the past fifteen years of getting out of the Army.

The ADRB can review most discharges, including Bad Conduct discharges issued as part of a Special Court-Martial. However, they cannot review Bad Conduct or Dishonorable Discharges issued as part of a General Court-Martial sentence.

The ADRB's empowerment is limited to upgrading a discharge and the reason for the discharge. Their empowerment does not extend to changing re-enlistment (RE) codes or otherwise modifying the contents of a veteran's military record.

Applicants can choose either a personal appearance-type hearing before a Review Board or a non-personal appearance review, which considers the available medical and administrative records as well as any supporting documentation submitted with the application.

Many times an applicant will apply for a non-appearance type of hearing first and if unsuccessful, then ask for a personal appearance type of hearing. Statistically, personal appearance type hearings have a much higher rate of success.

If the applicant chooses non-appearance hearing first, and is unsuccessful, then asks for a personal appearance-type hearing, they have the advantage of getting their discharge case reviewed twice. Because a personal appearance hearing must be made within 15-years of discharge, it is imperative to plan enough in advance so there is time for both the non-personal and personal hearings to occur before the fifteen years have passed.

DD Form 293

This form is used as an application to the Army Discharge Review Board. It's available online at arba.army.pentagon.mil/documents/dd0293.pdf

APPLICATION FOR THE REVIEW OF DISCHARGE OR DISMISSAL FROM THE ARMED FORCES OF THE UNITED STATES *(Please read instructions on Pages 3 and 4 BEFORE completing this application.)*	Form Approved OMB No. 0704-0004 Expires Aug 31, 2006

The public reporting burden for this collection of information is estimated to average 30 minutes per response, including the time for reviewing instructions, searching existing data sources, gathering and maintaining the data needed, and completing and reviewing the collection of information. Send comments regarding this burden estimate or any other aspect of this collection of information, including suggestions for reducing the burden, to Department of Defense, Washington Headquarters Services, Directorate for Information Operations and Reports (0704-0004), 1215 Jefferson Davis Highway, Suite 1204, Arlington, VA 22302-4302. Respondents should be aware that notwithstanding any other provision of law, no person shall be subject to any penalty for failing to comply with a collection of information if it does not display a currently valid OMB control number.
PLEASE DO NOT RETURN YOUR FORM TO THE ABOVE ADDRESS. RETURN COMPLETED FORM TO THE APPROPRIATE ADDRESS ON BACK OF THIS PAGE.

PRIVACY ACT STATEMENT
AUTHORITY: 10 U.S.C. 1553; E.O. 9397.
PRINCIPAL PURPOSE(S): To apply for a change in the characterization or reason for military discharge issued to an individual.
ROUTINE USE(S): None.
DISCLOSURE: Voluntary; however, failure to provide identifying information may impede processing of this application. The request for Social Security Number is strictly to assure proper identification of the individual and appropriate records.

1. APPLICANT DATA *(The person whose discharge is to be reviewed).* PLEASE PRINT OR TYPE INFORMATION.

a. BRANCH OF SERVICE (X one)	ARMY	MARINE CORPS	NAVY	AIR FORCE	COAST GUARD
b. NAME (Last, First, Middle Initial)		c. GRADE/RANK AT DISCHARGE		d. SOCIAL SECURITY NUMBER	

2. DATE OF DISCHARGE OR SEPARATION (YYYYMMDD) (If date is more than 15 years ago, submit a DD Form 149)	4. DISCHARGE CHARACTERIZATION RECEIVED (X one)	5. BOARD ACTION REQUESTED (X one)
	HONORABLE	CHANGE TO HONORABLE
	GENERAL/UNDER HONORABLE CONDITIONS	CHANGE TO GENERAL/UNDER HONORABLE CONDITIONS
	UNDER OTHER THAN HONORABLE CONDITIONS	CHANGE TO UNCHARACTERIZED (Not applicable for Air Force)
3. UNIT AND LOCATION AT DISCHARGE OR SEPARATION	BAD CONDUCT (Special court-martial only)	CHANGE NARRATIVE REASON FOR SEPARATION TO:
	UNCHARACTERIZED	
	OTHER (Explain)	

6. ISSUES: WHY AN UPGRADE OR CHANGE IS REQUESTED AND JUSTIFICATION FOR THE REQUEST *(Continue in Item 14. See instructions on Page 3.)*

7. (X if applicable) AN APPLICATION WAS PREVIOUSLY SUBMITTED ON (YYYYMMDD) AND THIS FORM IS SUBMITTED TO ADD ADDITIONAL ISSUES, JUSTIFICATION, OR EVIDENCE.

8. IN SUPPORT OF THIS APPLICATION, THE FOLLOWING ATTACHED DOCUMENTS ARE SUBMITTED AS EVIDENCE: *(Continue in Item 17. If military documents or medical records are relevant to your case, please send copies.)*

9. TYPE OF REVIEW REQUESTED (X one)

	CONDUCT A RECORD REVIEW OF MY DISCHARGE BASED ON MY MILITARY PERSONNEL FILE AND ANY ADDITIONAL DOCUMENTATION SUBMITTED BY ME. I AND/OR (counsel/representative) WILL NOT APPEAR BEFORE THE BOARD.
	I AND/OR (counsel/representative) WISH TO APPEAR AT A HEARING AT NO EXPENSE TO THE GOVERNMENT BEFORE THE BOARD IN THE WASHINGTON, D.C. METROPOLITAN AREA.
	I AND/OR (counsel/representative) WISH TO APPEAR AT A HEARING AT NO EXPENSE TO THE GOVERNMENT BEFORE A TRAVELING PANEL CLOSEST TO (enter city and state) (NOTE: The Navy Discharge Review Board does not have a traveling panel.)

10.a. COUNSEL/REPRESENTATIVE (If any) NAME (Last, First, Middle Initial) AND ADDRESS (See Item 10 of the instructions about counsel/representative.)	b. TELEPHONE NUMBER (Include Area Code)
	c. E-MAIL
	d. FAX NUMBER (Include Area Code)

11. APPLICANT MUST SIGN IN ITEM 13.a. BELOW. If the record in question is that of a deceased or incompetent person, LEGAL PROOF OF DEATH OR INCOMPETENCY MUST ACCOMPANY THE APPLICATION. If the application is signed by other than the applicant, indicate the name (print) _____ and relationship by marking a box below.

SPOUSE	WIDOW	WIDOWER	NEXT OF KIN	LEGAL REPRESENTATIVE	OTHER (Specify)

12.a. CURRENT MAILING ADDRESS OF APPLICANT OR PERSON ABOVE (Forward notification of any change in address.)	b. TELEPHONE NUMBER (Include Area Code)
	c. E-MAIL
	d. FAX NUMBER (Include Area Code)

13. CERTIFICATION. I make the foregoing statements, as part of my claim, with full knowledge of the penalties involved for willfully making a false statement or claim. (U.S. Code, Title 18, Sections 287 and 1001, provide that an individual shall be fined under this title or imprisoned not more than 5 years, or both.)	CASE NUMBER (Do not write in this space.)
a. SIGNATURE - REQUIRED (Applicant or person in Item 11 above)	b. DATE SIGNED - REQUIRED (YYYYMMDD)

DD FORM 293, AUG 2003	PREVIOUS EDITIONS ARE OBSOLETE.	Reset	Page 1 of 4 Pages

Instructions for filling out DD Form 293

Item 1 - Applicant Data

- Item 1a - Branch of Service. Mark the box in front of Army.
- Item 1b. - Enter your Last Name, First Name, Middle Initial that you were using at the time of your discharge.
- If you changed your name after discharge, enter your current name and the abbreviation "AKA" with the name you were using at the time of your discharge after that.
- If the former member is deceased or incompetent, see Item 11.
- Item 1c - Enter your grade or rank at the time of discharge.
- Item 1d - Enter your Social Security Number.

Item 2 – Date of Discharge. If you have multiple discharges, enter the date of discharge that you want changed. **Note:** Discharge Review Boards cannot consider any type of discharge resulting from a sentence given by a general court-martial.

Item 3 – Enter your Unit or your location at time of discharge or separation. **Note:** If your discharge was issued over fifteen years ago, petition the Army Board of Corrections for Military Records and use DD Form 149.

Item 4 - Mark the appropriate box of the discharge characterization received.

Item 5 – Mark the appropriate block for the action you are requesting.

Item 6 - Clearly state why an upgrade is requested and the justification for the request. Focus on the reasons you believe the discharge was either improper or inequitable. If you need more room, continue in Item 14.

Item 7 – Mark the box if you have already submitted an application or if you are submitting additional issues, justifications, or evidence. If you already submitted an application, enter the date in YYYYMMDD format.

Item 8 – List the supporting documentation you are submitting with the application.

Item 9 – Mark the box for the type of review you are requesting. **Note 1**: A discharge review is conducted in two basic ways:

• Records Review – The board conducts a discharge review based solely on military records and any additional supporting documentation that you provide. This review is conducted without personal appearance by you or your counsel.
• Hearing - You may appear before the board alone or with counsel in the Washington, D.C. Metro Area, or before a traveling board panel that stops in selected locations throughout the U.S.

Note 2: Failure to appear at a hearing or to respond to a scheduling notice, without making a prior timely request for a continuance, postponement, or withdrawal of your application, forfeits your right to a personal appearance. The board will complete its review of your discharge based upon the evidence of record and not on your or your counsel's appearance.

Item 10 – Counsel/Representative

- Item 10a – If you do have counsel/representation, enter their Last Name, First Name, Middle Initial. If you do not have counsel/representation, leave blank along with Items 10b through 10d.
- Item 10b - Enter counsel/representative's telephone number with area code.
- Item 10c - Enter counsel/representative's email address.
- Item 10d - Enter counsel/representative's fax number with area code.

Note: If you later obtain the services of either, inform the Board immediately.

Item 11 - Print the name of the person submitting the form on behalf of the military member and mark the appropriate box of the relationship to the soldier/veteran.

If the member is deceased or incompetent, the form may be submitted by a surviving spouse, next of kin, or legal representative.

Note: Copies of legal proof of death or incompetency, and evidence of the relationship to the former member, must be included with the application.

Item 12 – Current mailing address of the applicant or person submitting the application, and on Item 12a you should enter the current address of the applicant or the person in Item 11 submitting the application.

Item 12b – Enter surviving spouse, next of kin or representative's telephone number with area code.

- Item 12c – Enter surviving spouse, next of kin or representative's email address.
- Item 12d - Enter surviving spouse, next of kin or representative's fax number with area code. If no fax number is available, leave blank.

Note: If you change this address while this application is pending, you must notify the Discharge Review Board immediately. Failure to attend a hearing as a result of an unreported change in address may result in your waiving your right to a hearing.

Item 13 – Certification – By signing, the applicant or person in Item 11 understands the penalties for making false statements.

- Item 13a – Signature of the applicant or person in Item 11.
- Item 13b – Enter the date the form is signed in YYYYMMDD format.

A Discharge Upgrade through the ADRB

An ADRB application to request a discharge upgrade starts with DD Form 293 - Application for the Review of Discharge or Dismissal from the Armed Forces of the United States. (See Chapter 7). There are five basic ways to fill out an application:

- Online;
- Download from the Internet;
- Pick up a copy at any Department of Defense (DoD) installation;
- Pick up a copy from any regional VA office;
- Request in writing from:

The Army Review Boards Agency (ARBA)
1901 South Bell Street, 2nd Floor
Arlington VA 22202-4508

or call them at 703-607-1600

Complete the form by typing or legibly writing in the information. The online option is in a fillable format and you can print it after it's filled out.

Item 6 on the form is very important. In the space provided, you must separately list the specific issues supporting the upgrade you are asking the board to consider and resolve. Once you have finished completing the form and making copies of your supporting documentation that you will send with the form, mail the form to the address shown on the form. Ensure you sign the form in Item 13.

Supporting Your Request

When considering your request for an upgrade, the board considers only whether your current discharge was inequitable or improper – that's it. Because this is only what they look at, it is your responsibility to prove how your discharge is inequitable or improper. You make your proof by providing evidence to support your charge, such as signed statements from you or your witnesses, or copies of documents you wish to submit.

Witness statements must be signed by a notary. Just providing names of people you would like to use as witnesses is not sufficient evidence; the board will not contact these people for you for their statements – this is something you must do and you must attach their statements to your application form.

When gathering evidence to support your discharge upgrade claim, look to the people who best knew your military service, such as people in your rating chain, your First Sergeant and Commander, or subordinates who may have been under your control.

What you did after you got out is of no interest of the board. They want to know what you did while you were in – and especially during the time that caused the Army to give you your current discharge. Only you can best determine which evidence will best support your case for an upgrade. Remember, keep your focus on proving how your discharge was either inequitable or improper. Don't get off track.

Depending on how much evidence you have, and from how many people you attempt to get it, it will take some time for these people to write up their support and get their documentation back to you. You might also want to get a copy of your Military Record from the National Personnel Records Center to submit with your application. You can request a copy of your records by submitting **Standard Form 180.**

The point is: This all takes time. You want everything attached to your DD Form 293 when you send in your packet. It is important to ensure you start the process of gathering evidence far enough in advance that you can get everything together and submitted well in advance of the 15-year deadline.

If you choose to make a personal appearance, be sure to check Item 4 on your DD Form 293. If you do, the Board will notify you of the date, time, and place for your hearing. Generally, it will take place in Washington D.C, but boards do travel occasionally to specified cities when enough cases are in an area to make it worthwhile for the travel expense involved.

You Are Not Alone: The ADRB considers almost all discharges except punitive discharges issued by a courts-martial. So if your discharge is something other than punitive, the board should be able to consider it. While most applicants try to go through the process on their own, there are resources available to help you should you choose to use them. Some are free, while others you will have to pay for.

If you don't understand the process, these resources can assist or represent you:

- Veterans' service organizations - Many of these organizations, such as the American Legion or Veterans of Foreign Wars, have people on staff to help you complete the paperwork or represent you at the board.
- Personal Lawyer – There are many lawyers specializing in discharge upgrade cases who are willing to help you; however, you must pay for their services.

If you choose to use counsel or a representative, be sure to list the person and contact information in Item 10 a-d on your DD Form 293. If you name a representative, the board will normally deal directly with your representative instead of with you.

Even if you choose not to have a veterans' service organization represent you, they will still be willing to advise you as you prepare your application or for your board appearance. You can also ask questions of the board in writing, and one of their staff members will respond with answers.

Two things will best increase your chances to get your discharge upgraded – a personal appearance by you at the hearing, and hiring an attorney specializing in discharge review processes. Yes, with a personal appearance and counsel representation, you will have expenses involved, but if you are serious about getting your discharge changed, these are the best two things you can do toward accomplishing that mission; it can also be the best money you will ever spend.

Sending in Your Discharge Upgrade Packet

Mail your completed packet to:
Army Review Boards Agency
Support Division, St. Louis
9700 Page Avenue
ATTN: SFMR-RBR-SL
St. Louis MO 63132-5200

The ADRB does not directly change Reenlistment Codes (RE Codes). However, if upgrading a discharge affects your current RE code, they will also consider upgrading your RE code to one that can be waivered, so you could enlist back in one of the service branches. If you just want to have your RE Code upgraded, then you should appeal to the Army Board of Corrections to Military Records and not the Army Discharge Review Board.

The ADRB Process

If you requested a personal appearance before the board (by checking Item 4 on DD Form 293), the board will notify you of the time, date, and place of the hearing. They normally meet in Washington, D.C. However, there are times when they will travel to various regional locations to conduct hearings.

All expenses you incur to meet before the board are borne by you. The government will not reimburse you or pay for travel and lodging (or counsel and witness fees if you choose to use these as resources/evidence).

If after being notified in writing of the time and place of the hearing, you fail to appear either in person or by representation, or if you did not make a prior timely request for a continuation, postponement, or withdrawal, you will waive your right to a hearing and the Army Discharge Review Board will proceed with a records review to determine whether you warrant an upgrade. The only way another hearing will be granted is if you can prove you missed your first hearing due to circumstances beyond your control.

Your board hearing is administrative in nature, and its sole purpose is to determine whether your period of service was properly characterized. The burden of proof that the characterization was wrong lies with you or the person submitting the application on your behalf. In other words, it is your responsibility to prove to the board that the characterization you currently have is wrong – and why it is wrong. If you cannot do that, your effort for a discharge upgrade will fail.

In the personal appearance hearing, the ADRB allows you representation by either a lawyer or non-lawyer counsel. A board proceeding usually begins with opening remarks by your counsel (if you have any) followed by your counsel's asking questions directly of you. Then, board members will ask you questions and a closing statement will be made by your counsel. Applicants may also request witnesses to testify at hearings.

If you choose a board appearance, it is advisable that you review the examiner's brief, which is an easy-to-read summary of your military records, to determine whether all the facts in the brief are correct. One board member will be designated the Actions Officer. Should the board have questions concerning the documentation in your record either during or after the hearing, it is the Actions Officer's job to produce the document in question and resolve the issue.

Your hearing will be recorded at the start of the proceedings; you may get a copy of it after the proceedings are finished just by asking for it.

Then, the Board President calls the board to order. The Action Officer states for the recording that you are present (if you are), whether you have counsel present, and whether you plan to introduce any evidence in the proceedings. Next, you are asked what kind of testimony, if any, you wish to give. During the hearing, you can remain silent or give either sworn or un-sworn testimony.

If you chose to give sworn testimony, you will be sworn in before giving your testimony. The whole hearing normally takes about an hour; however, there is no time limit. Each board member casts one vote and decisions by the board are on a majority-rules basis. In six to eight weeks, you will get the board's decision.

If you were fortunate enough to have your discharge upgraded, then you will get a new discharge certificate, updated DD Form 214, and a copy of the decision paperwork. If your discharge was not upgraded, you will get a copy of the decision paperwork, the reason(s) your discharge was not upgraded, and any follow-on appeals you may be authorized to file.

The Army Board for Correction of Military Records

The Army Board for Correction of Military Records (ABCMR) differs from the ADRB in that it consists of high ranking Army civilian employees. The ABCMR has much more power in that they can change, delete, modify, or add to the contents of military records. As a matter of fact, the ABCMR can do anything to a veteran's record *except* overturn a court-martial conviction. In that regard, however, they can order a correction to a record showing they approved part of a sentence, but not a punitive discharge.

They convene only in Washington, D.C., and while they are not required to grant personal appearances (and rarely do), they can.

The ABCMR operates under a three-year timeline from date of discovery of the error or injustice, which differs from the ADRB's 15-year time limit. While the ADRB's time limit cannot be waived, the ABCMR's 3-year limit can be, if after making a cursory review it is considered "in the interest of justice" to do so.

For veterans past the 3-years-from-discovery date, they must explain in Item 6 of DD Form 149 why the board should still consider the case, since it is over the 3-year time limit. (See Chapter 11)

ABCMR decisions are binding and final for all federal agencies including the Veterans Administration. This is important in General Court-Martial cases where the discharge was a part of the sentence, because it then bars the veterans from using VA benefits.

If an ABCMR changes the reason for discharge from a General Court-Martial sentence to an action by the ABCMR, the discharge no longer is the result of a General Court-Martial and can remove the barrier to using VA benefits.

DD Form 149

This form is used to apply to the Army Board of Corrections of Military Records. It's online at: www.dtic.mil/whs/directives/infomgt/forms/eforms/dd0149.pdf

APPLICATION FOR CORRECTION OF MILITARY RECORD UNDER THE PROVISIONS OF TITLE 10, U.S. CODE, SECTION 1552 (Please read instructions on reverse side BEFORE completing this application.)	OMB No. 0704-0003

The public reporting burden for this collection of information is estimated to average 30 minutes per response, including the time for reviewing instructions, searching existing data sources, gathering and maintaining the data needed, and completing and reviewing the collection of information. Send comments regarding this burden estimate or any other aspect of this collection of information, including suggestions for reducing the burden, to the Department of Defense, Executive Services Directorate, Information Management Division, 1155 Defense Pentagon, Washington, DC 20301-1155 (0704-0003). Respondents should be aware that notwithstanding any other provision of law, no person shall be subject to any penalty for failing to comply with a collection of information if it does not display a currently valid OMB control number.

PLEASE DO NOT RETURN YOUR COMPLETED FORM TO THE ABOVE ORGANIZATION. RETURN COMPLETED FORM TO THE APPROPRIATE ADDRESS ON THE BACK OF THIS PAGE.

PRIVACY ACT STATEMENT

AUTHORITY: Title 10 US Code 1552, EO 9397.

ROUTINE USE(S): None.

PRINCIPAL PURPOSE: To initiate an application for correction of military record. The form is used by Board members for review of pertinent information in making a determination of relief through correction of a military record.

DISCLOSURE: Voluntary; however, failure to provide identifying information may impede processing of this application. The request for Social Security number is strictly to assure proper identification of the individual and appropriate records.

1. APPLICANT DATA (The person whose record you are requesting to be corrected.)

a. BRANCH OF SERVICE (X one)	ARMY	NAVY	AIR FORCE	MARINE CORPS	COAST GUARD
b. NAME (Print - Last, First, Middle Initial)		c. PRESENT OR LAST PAY GRADE	d. SERVICE NUMBER (If applicable)	e. SSN	

2. PRESENT STATUS WITH RESPECT TO THE ARMED SERVICES (Active Duty, Reserve, National Guard, Retired, Discharged, Deceased)	3. TYPE OF DISCHARGE (If by court-martial, state the type of court.)	4. DATE OF DISCHARGE OR RELEASE FROM ACTIVE DUTY (YYYYMMDD)

5. I REQUEST THE FOLLOWING ERROR OR INJUSTICE IN THE RECORD BE CORRECTED: (Entry required)

6. I BELIEVE THE RECORD TO BE IN ERROR OR UNJUST FOR THE FOLLOWING REASONS: (Entry required)

7. ORGANIZATION AND APPROXIMATE DATE (YYYYMMDD) AT THE TIME THE ALLEGED ERROR OR INJUSTICE IN THE RECORD OCCURRED (Entry required)

8. DISCOVERY OF ALLEGED ERROR OR INJUSTICE

a. DATE OF DISCOVERY (YYYYMMDD)	b. IF MORE THAN THREE YEARS SINCE THE ALLEGED ERROR OR INJUSTICE WAS DISCOVERED, STATE WHY THE BOARD SHOULD FIND IT IN THE INTEREST OF JUSTICE TO CONSIDER THE APPLICATION.

9. IN SUPPORT OF THIS APPLICATION, I SUBMIT AS EVIDENCE THE FOLLOWING ATTACHED DOCUMENTS: (If military documents or medical records are pertinent to your case, please send copies. If Veterans Affairs records are pertinent, give regional office location and claim number.)

10. I DESIRE TO APPEAR BEFORE THE BOARD IN WASHINGTON, D.C. (At no expense to the Government) (X one)	YES. THE BOARD WILL DETERMINE IF WARRANTED.	NO. CONSIDER MY APPLICATION BASED ON RECORDS AND EVIDENCE.

11.a. COUNSEL (If any) NAME (Last, First, Middle Initial) and ADDRESS (Include ZIP Code)	b. TELEPHONE (Include Area Code)
	c. E-MAIL ADDRESS
	d. FAX NUMBER (Include Area Code)

12. APPLICANT MUST SIGN IN ITEM 15 BELOW. If the record in question is that of a deceased or incompetent person, LEGAL PROOF OF DEATH OR INCOMPETENCY MUST ACCOMPANY THE APPLICATION. If the application is signed by other than the applicant, indicate the name (print) and relationship by marking one box below.

SPOUSE	WIDOW	WIDOWER	NEXT OF KIN	LEGAL REPRESENTATIVE	OTHER (Specify)

13.a. COMPLETE CURRENT ADDRESS (Include ZIP Code) OF APPLICANT OR PERSON IN ITEM 12 ABOVE (Forward notification of all changes of address.)	b. TELEPHONE (Include Area Code)
	c. E-MAIL ADDRESS
	d. FAX NUMBER (Include Area Code)

14. I MAKE THE FOREGOING STATEMENTS, AS PART OF MY CLAIM, WITH FULL KNOWLEDGE OF THE PENALTIES INVOLVED FOR WILLFULLY MAKING A FALSE STATEMENT OR CLAIM. (U.S. Code, Title 18, Sections 287 and 1001, provide that an individual shall be fined under this title or imprisoned not more than 5 years, or both.)	CASE NUMBER (Do not write in this space.)
15. SIGNATURE (Applicant must sign here.)	16. DATE SIGNED (YYYYMMDD)

DD FORM 149, JUN 2010   PREVIOUS EDITION IS OBSOLETE.   Adobe Designer 9.0

Instructions for filling out DD Form 149

Item 1 - Applicant Data

- Item 1a - Branch of Service. Mark the box in front of Army.
- Item 1b. - Enter your Last Name, First Name, Middle Initial that you were using at the time of your discharge.
- If you changed your name after discharge, enter your current name and the abbreviation "AKA" after it, along with your previous name.
- If the former member is deceased or incompetent, see Item 11.
- Item 1c - Enter your present or last pay grade.
- Item 1d - Enter your Service Number (if you have one, otherwise leave blank.)
- Item 1e - Enter your Social Security Number.

Item 2 – Enter your status with the Armed Forces for the discharge you wish to have changed.

Note: The ADRB cannot consider any type of discharge resulting from a sentence given by a general court-martial.

Item 3 – Enter your type of discharge. **Note:** If discharged by court-martial, enter the type of court.

Item 4 – Enter date of discharge or separation in YYYYMMDD format.

Item 5 – Enter the error or injustice in your record you wish to have corrected.

Item 6 - Clearly state why an upgrade is requested and the justification for the request. Focus on the reasons you believe the discharge was either in error or an injustice.

Item 7 – Enter your unit at the time the error or injustice occurred, and the date in YYYYMMDD format.

Item 8 – Discovery of Alleged Error or Injustice

- Item 8a – Enter date of discovery in YYYYMMDD format.
- Item 8 b – If three years have passed since discovery, tell the board why they should consider your request.

Item 9 – List the supporting evidence you are submitting with your application.

Item 10 – Mark the appropriate box stating whether you wish to appear before the board. **Note 1:** Failure to appear at a hearing or respond to a scheduling notice without a prior timely request for a continuance, postponement, or withdrawal of the application will forfeit your right to a personal appearance. The board will complete its review based upon the evidence in record and packet – and without your or your counsel's appearance.

Item 11 - Counsel/Representative

- Item 11a – If you have counsel/representation, enter their Last Name, First Name, Middle Initial. If you have none, leave blank along with Items 11b through 11d.

- Item 11b - Enter counsel/representative's telephone number with area code.
- Item 11c - Enter counsel/representative's email address.
- Item 11d . Enter counsel/representative's fax number with area code.

Item 12 - Print the name of the person submitting the form on behalf of the veteran and mark the appropriate box of the relationship to the veteran. If the veteran for which the form is being submitted is deceased or incompetent, the form may be submitted by a surviving spouse, next of kin, or legal representative. **Note:** Copies of legal proof of death or incompetency, and evidence of the relationship to the former member, must be included with the application.

Item 13 - Current mailing address of the applicant or person submitting the application.

- Item 13a – Enter current address of applicant or the person in Item 11 submitting the application.
- Item 13b – Enter surviving spouse, next of kin, or representative's telephone number with area code.
- Item 13c – Enter surviving spouse, next of kin, or representative's email address.
- Item 13d - Enter surviving spouse, next of kin, or representative's fax number with area code.

Note: If you change this address while this application is pending, you must notify the board immediately. Failure to attend a hearing as a result of an unreported change in address may result in a waiver of your right to a hearing.

Item 14 – By signing, you or the person in Item 11 understands the penalties for making false statements.

Item 15 – Signature of the applicant or person in Item 11.

Item 16 – Enter the date the form is signed in YYYYMMDD format.

A Discharge Upgrade through the ABCMR

An ABCMR application to request a discharge upgrade starts with DD Form 149 - Application for the Correction of Military Records. (See Chapter 11). Like the DD Form 293, there are five basic ways to get a copy of the form:

- Online;
- Download from the Internet;
- Pick up a copy at any Department of Defense (DoD) installation;
- Pick up a copy from any regional VA office;
- Request in writing from:

the Army Review Boards Agency (ARBA)
1901 South Bell Street, 2nd Floor
Arlington VA 22202-4508

or call them at 703-607-1600

Complete the form either by typing or legibly writing in the information. The online option is in a fillable format; you can print it after it's filled out.

Item 9 on the form is very important. In the space provided you must, in simple terms, describe the error and why you think it is an error. You can continue in Item 17 or on the back of the form if necessary, or type up your statement on plain white paper. You are allowed up to 25 pages of supporting documentation.

Once you have finished completing the form and making copies of your supporting documentation, mail the form to the address shown on the form. Ensure you sign in Item 15.

Supporting Your Request

While the ADRB considers whether your discharge was improper or inequitable, the ABCMR considers whether an error or injustice was made in your discharge rating. You make your proof by providing evidence to support your charge, such as signed statements from you or your witnesses or copies of documents you wish to submit. Remember, documents from witnesses must be signed by a notary. Just as with DD Form 293, providing names of people you would like to use as witnesses is not sufficient evidence; the board will not chase down these people for their statements – it is something you must do.

Item 8b on DD Form 149 is also an important block if it has been more than 3 years since you discovered that an error was made. In this block, you have to explain why the board should still consider your application, even though you did not submit it within the required 3-year timeframe of discovery. In other words, you must explain why you waited so long to submit an application after discovering the error. Write it out as clearly and simply as you can.

Just like for the ADRB, when gathering your evidence to support your ABCMR claim, look to the people who best knew your military service, such as people in your rating chain, your First

Sergeant and Commander, or subordinates who may have been under your control.

Many people think what they have done since they got out will impress the board. But the board members want to know what you did while you were in, and especially during the time that caused the Army to give you your current discharge. Only you can determine which evidence will best support your case for a change to your discharge. Remember, keep your focus on proving how your discharge was in error or was an injustice. Don't get off track and lose your focus.

Depending on how much evidence and from how many people you intend to collect it to support your case, it will take some time to contact them, and for them to write up their support and get it back to you. You might also want to get a copy of your Military Record from the National Personnel Records Center by submitting Standard Form 180 to include with your application.

The point is: All this takes time. You want everything attached to your DD Form 149 when you send in your packet. Be sure you start the evidence-gathering process far enough in advance that you can get everything together and submitted well before the 3-year deadline.

If you request to make a personal appearance by checking Item 6 on your DD Form 149, the board will decide whether a personal appearance is necessary. Generally, personal appearances are not required, which is more reason for you to present your case as clearly and completely as possible on paper. You should assume that you or your counsel/representative will not get a chance to plead your case in person. In other words, don't give the board a chance to dismiss your case because your packet was lacking something and incomplete.

If a personal appearance is granted, the board will give you the details. This board normally meets in Washington D.C., and all travel expenses for you, your witnesses, and counsel/representation are on your own dime.

Once the board receives your application packet, it will request an advisory opinion from the Army. If the advisory opinion comes back not recommending a change, you will be provided a copy of the opinion and 30 days to make comments regarding the opinion. Generally, an additional 30 days can be granted by requesting it, if you need the extra time for your comments. Keep in mind, this is only an opinion and only part of what the board will use to make a final decision.

If you have nothing further to say, you do not have to respond to the opinion. Not responding will neither increase nor decrease your chances for a fair hearing. It just means you have nothing else to say about the issue.

Help Is Available

Like the ADRB, the ABCMR considers almost all discharges, but this board can review punitive discharges issued by a courts-martial as well. So if your discharge is punitive, this is the board to consider your case. Most applicants try to negotiate the process by themselves; however, just as with the ADRB, many of the same resources are available to help you if you choose to use them. Basically they are the same as those for the ADRB:

- Veterans' service organizations - Many of these organizations, such as the American Legion or Veterans of Foreign Wars, have people on staff to help you complete the paperwork before sending it to the board.
- Personal Lawyer – There are many lawyers specializing in discharge upgrade cases who are willing to help you prepare your case; however, you must pay for their services.

If you choose to use counsel or a representative, be sure to name that person and their contact information in Item 11 on your DD Form 293. If you name a representative, the board will normally deal directly with your representative instead of with you if they need information.

Two things will best increase your chances to get your error changed – your willingness to make a personal board appearance, and hiring an attorney specializing in correction of military records. Just note that you will have expenses involved if you have to travel to the board or hire an attorney. But if you want to get your error or injustice changed, this gives you the best chance to get it changed.

Sending in Your DD Form 149 Packet

Once you have gathered up all your evidence and completed DD Form 149, you can mail your packet to:

Army Review Boards Agency
Support Division, St. Louis
ATTN: SFMR-RBR-SL
9700 Page Avenue
St. Louis MO 63132-5200

The ABCMR Board Process

The Secretary of the Army appoints approximately 90 Army civilians to the ABCMR board pool as an additional duty. Three members at a time are randomly selected from this pool and assigned to a specific board.

Records are reviewed on a first-come, first-served basis. ABCMR staff members prepare the records ahead of time for the Board to review. Staff members also serve as technical advisers to board members should something require clarification from a laws/regulations standpoint.

The board meets in closed session and will make a recommendation based on your packet, evidence in your official military record, and governing military law and regulations. They make a recommendation on a majority-rules basis. The dissenting member may submit a minority opinion to the Secretary of the Army, but this is not required.

The recommendation then goes to the Deputy Assistant Secretary of the Army, who approves or disapproves the Board's recommendation on behalf of the Secretary of the Army. This Board is the highest administrative appeal level and is the final decision as far as the Army is concerned.

Once the recommendation is accepted or denied, you will receive a letter informing you of the decision. If the decision is favorable, the board also contacts DFAS to see if any pay is due you based on the decision.

Glossary

Board for the Correction of Military Records – Generally, a non-appearance board with the power to correct veterans' records and upgrade discharges within three years of the date of discovery.

Civilian Conviction - Conviction by civilian authorities or action taken that is tantamount to a finding of guilty and includes confinement for 6 months or more without regard to suspension or probation.

Commission of a Serious Offense - Commission of a serious military or civilian offense if the specific circumstances of the offense warrant separation or a punitive discharge.

DD Form 149 - This form is used as an application to have a discharge reviewed by the Discharge Review Board.

DD Form 293 - This form is used as an application to have a discharge reviewed by the Army Board of Correction of Military Records.

Discharge – The end of one's military service.

Discharge Review Board – Reviews most discharges within 15 years of discharge except Bad Conduct or Dishonorable Discharges issued as part of a General Court-Martial sentence.

Enuresis - Bed-wetting

Homosexual Act – an attempted, solicited, or committed homosexual act in the following circumstances:

- By force, coercion, or intimidation;
- With a person under 16 years of age;

- With a subordinate that violates superior-subordinate relationships;
- In public view;
- For compensation;
- Aboard a military vessel or aircraft; or
- In another location having an adverse impact on discipline, good order or morale.

Improper - The reason or characterization of the discharge is in error.

Inequitable - The reason or characterization of the discharge is not consistent with the policies and traditions of the service.

Minor Disciplinary Infractions - A pattern of misconduct consisting solely of minor disciplinary infractions.

Pattern of Misconduct - A pattern of misconduct consisting of a discreditable involvement with civil or military authorities, or conduct prejudicial to good order and discipline.

Separation – The transfer from one military service to another. Soldiers who have served less than 8 years and get out of the Army are separated and placed in the IRR to finish out the 8-year military obligation.

Made in the USA
Columbia, SC
24 April 2021

36831547R00037